BLAZERS

MILITARY VEHICLES

★ ★ ★ ★ ★ ★ ★ ★ ★ ★ ★ ★ ★ ★ ★ ★

U.S.
ARMY
INFANTRY FIGHTING VEHICLES

by Martha E. H. Rustad

★ ★ ★ ★ ★ ★ ★ ★ ★ ★ ★ ★ ★ ★ ★ ★

Reading Consultant:
Barbara J. Fox
Reading Specialist
North Carolina State University

Capstone
press

Mankato, Minnesota

Blazers is published by Capstone Press,
151 Good Counsel Drive, P.O. Box 669, Mankato, Minnesota 56002.
www.capstonepress.com

Library of Congress Cataloging-in-Publication Data
Rustad, Martha E. H. (Martha Elizabeth Hillman), 1975–
    U.S. Army Infantry fighting vehicles / by Martha E. H. Rustad.
    p. cm.—(Blazers. Military vehicles)
    Summary: "Describes U.S. Army Infantry Fighting Vehicles, including their
design, weapons, equipment, and uses"—Provided by publisher.
    Includes bibliographical references and index.
    ISBN-13: 978-0-7368-6454-1 (hardcover)
    ISBN-10: 0-7368-6454-7 (hardcover)
    1. M2 Bradley infantry fighting vehicle—Juvenile literature. I. Title.
II. Series.
UG446.5.R87 2007
623.7'475—dc22   2006004100

Editorial Credits
Jennifer Besel, editor; Thomas Emery, set designer; Ted Williams, book designer;
    Jo Miller, photo researcher/photo editor

Photo Credits
AP/Wide World Photos/Eckehard Schulz, 12; John Moore, 7
Check Six/Sam Sargent, 4–5, 10–11 (top), 18–19 (bottom), 22–23, 28–29
Corbis/Dallas Morning News/David Leeson, 18–19 (top); Sgt. Brian
    Cumper, 8–9
DVIC, 16–17/John Byerly, 12–13; SPC 5 Bobby Mathis, 10–11 (bottom)
Getty Images Inc./Larry W. Smith, 6; Scott Nelson, 14–15, 24–25, 26–27
Photo by Ted Carlson/Fotodynamics, cover, 20–21

**Capstone Press thanks Ron Kuykendall of TSM–Stryker/Bradley for his
assistance in preparing this book.**

1 2 3 4 5 6 11 10 09 08 07 06

TABLE OF CONTENTS

INFANTRY FIGHTING VEHICLES

A huge vehicle rumbles across the battlefield. Soldiers jump out the back and rush into battle. The vehicle looks like a tank, but it is really a Bradley infantry fighting vehicle.

The U.S. Army relies on Bradleys when it needs to send soldiers into battle. Crews inside Bradleys use weapons to protect soldiers and to fire at enemy targets.

DESIGN

Bradleys are big, heavy vehicles. Each one weighs as much as six elephants. Their power comes from a 600-horsepower engine.

TRACK

★ ★ ★ ★ ★ ★

Wide tracks help Bradleys travel over rough ground and sand. Not even deep water can stop a Bradley from moving forward.

BLAZER FACT

On new models, a float called a pontoon is inflated around the Bradley when it needs to cross rivers or lakes.

BLAZER FACT

M3 Bradleys are used on scouting missions. They carry two soldiers and extra equipment.

A Bradley carries up to seven soldiers, plus the crew. A ramp on the back folds down to let the soldiers in and out.

When enemies fire weapons at Bradleys, thick metal armor protects the soldiers inside. The armor weighs about 6,000 pounds (2,700 kilograms).

WEAPONS AND EQUIPMENT

Bradleys can launch missiles at enemy targets. The TOW antitank missile can reach speeds of 761 miles (1,225 kilometers) per hour.

★ ★ ★ ★ ★ ★

Bradleys are also armed with an M242 Bushmaster chain gun. As many as 200 shots blast out of this gun each minute.

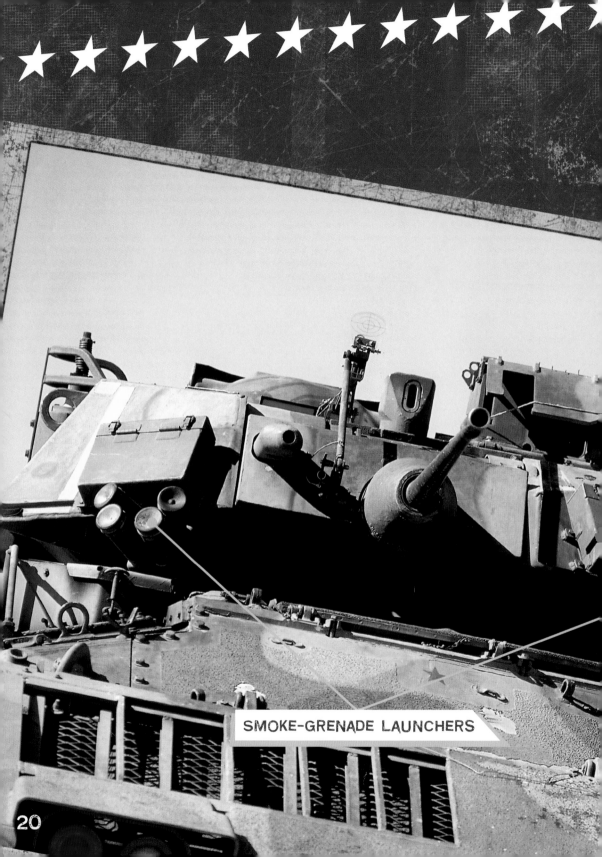

SMOKE-GRENADE LAUNCHERS

Bradleys have two smoke-grenade launchers. The crew uses the smoke to hide the Bradley from enemies.

M2A2 BRADLEY

TURRET

SMOKE-GRENADE LAUNCHER

HULL

TROOP COMPARTMENT DOOR

M242 BUSHMASTER CHAIN GUN

TOW ANTITANK MISSILE LAUNCHER

TRACKS

THE CREW AND ITS MISSIONS

Three crew members control a Bradley. The commander gives orders. The gunner loads and fires the weapons. The driver steers.

The U.S. Army depends on Bradleys to complete dangerous missions. The Bradley's mighty power helps soldiers get their jobs done.

RUMBLING INTO BATTLE!

GLOSSARY

armor (AR-mur)—a protective metal covering

missile (MISS-uhl)—an explosive weapon that can travel long distances

mission (MISH-uhn)—a military task

pontoon (pon-TOON)—a float that helps a boat or vehicle stay above water

scout (SKOUT)—to look or search for something

target (TAR-git)—something that is aimed at or shot at

track (TRAK)—a flat, steel belt that connects to a vehicle's road wheels

READ MORE

Bartlett, Richard. *U.S. Army Fighting Vehicles.*
United States Armed Forces. Chicago:
Heinemann, 2004.

Green, Michael, and Gladys Green. *Infantry
Fighting Vehicles: The M2A2 Bradleys.* War
Machines. Mankato, Minn.: Capstone Press, 2004.

Souter, Gerry. *Battle Tanks: Power in the Field.*
Mighty Military Machines. Berkeley Heights,
N.J.: Enslow, 2006.

INTERNET SITES

FactHound offers a safe, fun way to find Internet sites
related to this book. All of the sites on FactHound have
been researched by our staff.

Here's how:
1. Visit *www.facthound.com*
2. Choose your grade level.
3. Type in this book ID **0736864547** for
   age-appropriate sites. You may also browse
   subjects by clicking on letters, or by clicking
   on pictures and words.
4. Click on the **Fetch It** button.

FactHound will fetch the best sites for you!

INDEX